Stardust, the story of us;

Written by:          Neil Dennehy
Illustrations:       Neil Dennehy and Valentart
Cover design:        Neil Dennehy

Audience:            3 years +

Hardcover ISBN      978-1-9162426-4-7
Ebook ISBN          978-1-9162426-5-4
Audiobook ISBN      978-1-9162426-6-1

Visit our website at:
www.highestpotential.ie

# *Stardust*

## the story of us

by Neil Dennehy

*For those who need reminding of just how special we all are*

Our story begins at the start of it all, with a beautiful spark, powerful yet small,
all by itself in a vast empty sea, with dreams of the future and what it could be

It started to stretch,
then it started to grow
Its tiniest pieces,
they started to glow

as they danced, and they spun,
oh what a sight
when they made the first stars
to light up the night!

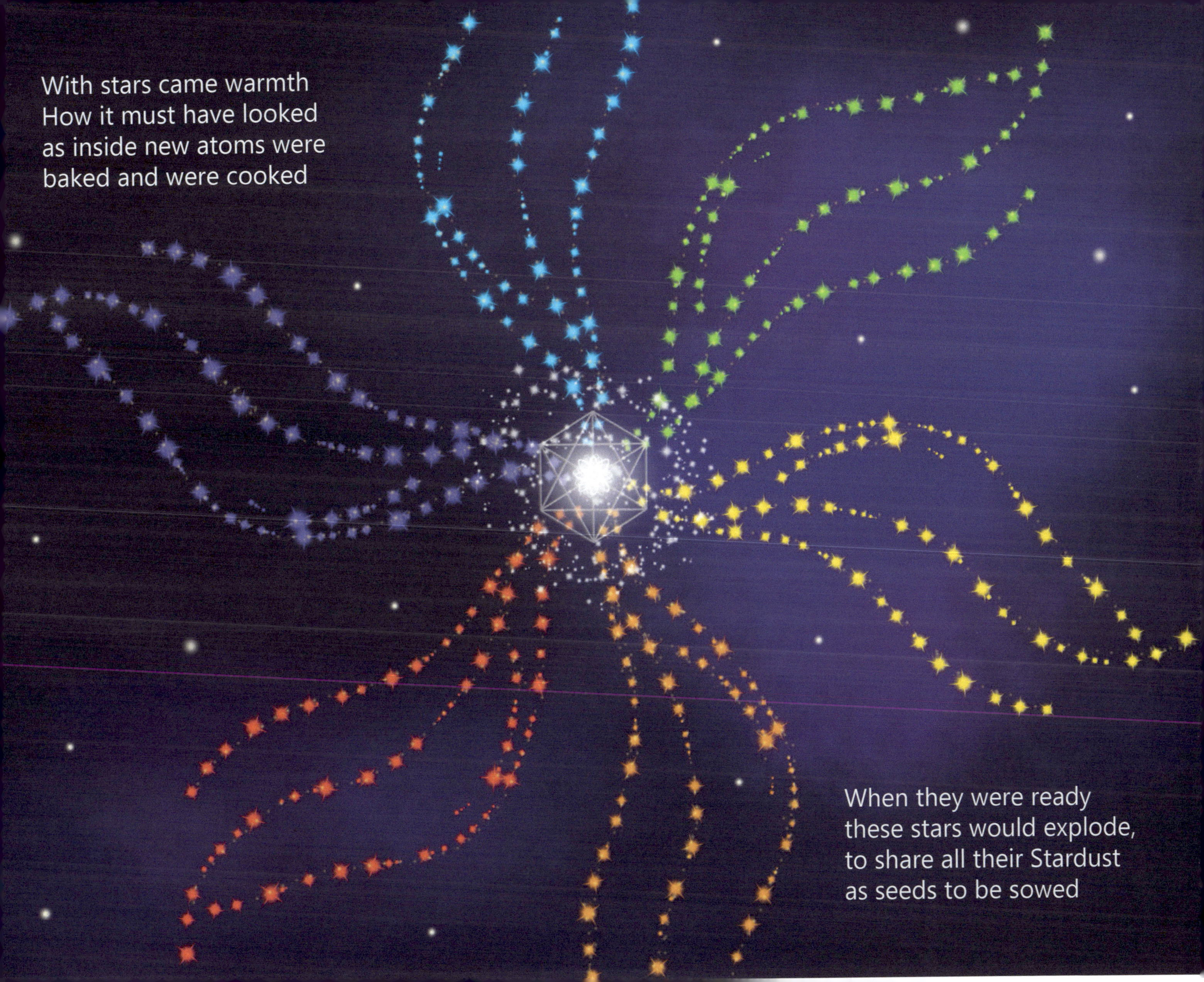
With stars came warmth
How it must have looked
as inside new atoms were
baked and were cooked

When they were ready
these stars would explode,
to share all their Stardust
as seeds to be sowed

This Stardust had plans,
such big dreams you see,
grown quite grand
from that spark's energy

With love at its core,
Stardust was free
and soon to become
all that would be

It formed into planets,
moons, stars, our sun
but life as we know it
had not yet begun

It had to make ready,
our world to prepare
for all of the creatures
that soon would live there

So it turned into land,
into skies, into seas,
plants in our oceans,
flowers and trees

with roots to connect
to the life-giving dirt,
they spread through the land
and clung to the earth

Then Stardust decided,
"I want so much more,
through the water I'll swim,
through the air I shall soar."

and it became birds,
reptiles, mammals and fish,
to live as it wanted,
to grant it's own wish

It grew into all sorts
and manners of creatures,
with all kinds of textures,
colours and features
to explore and experience
every sensation
on this beautiful world,
its own creation

Now as much as it loved
to swim, fly and walk,
Stardust decided
it wanted to talk
and since that was hard
with a snout or a beak,
it had an idea for
one that could speak

This one would be different. On earth it would walk,
but also would climb, run, jump, swim and talk!
When more of its kind learned to work together,
they'd fly in machines as light as a feather

2 + 3
8 - 5
14 + 54
8 : 4
With minds to imagine, voices to share
knowledge, ideas and hearts that would care
to help those who struggled to move, hear, were blind,
with love in their name, this new humankind

Becoming all people, all colours, all races,
and wanting to smile through so many faces,
it took on all shapes and sizes to be,
for Stardust adores variety

It loved being human, it had so much fun,
playing with friends in the warmth of the sun,
at night looking up at the stars high above,
reminded how all that we know came from Love

For all it became, Stardust never forgot
how it danced and played in a star's melting pot
All people, all creatures, our planet, our sun,
always connected, forever as one

That spark of creation still lies within
the core of each person and once we begin
to see that it's there, it's our power to use,
we'll make our dreams real however we choose

We'll care for our planet and for one another,
regardless of race, we are sisters and brothers,
building a world that fills us with pride
using the power of our Stardust inside

We'll leave our best work. That will surely inspire
those who come after to reach even higher,
proving why Stardust, with all of its might,
chose us as its dream and got us just right

This story began and though it is true, it has not yet ended, but it has led to you
So, live your whole life, shining brightly, you must, as the stars you are made of for
You are Stardust...

Keep shining!

Did you notice the Stardust smiles and hearts scattered throughout this book?

These are to remind you that joy and love are to be found everywhere,
if we choose to look for them!

## About the author

Neil Dennehy is a father of two children, Roma and Luca, for whom he would read bedtime stories at night, often making them up or adding in extra bits! He always enjoyed the positive messages and lessons contained within children's stories.

He began a career in Health and Wellness 22 years ago to live out his passion for helping people to feel good. He believes that everybody has value, purpose and potential and wrote this poem for those that have forgotten their worth. He has also published,"What to do with Stardust? to help his readers realise their potential as he loves to see people shine!

Visit www.highestpotential.ie for more of his work

## About the illustrators

Neil Dennehy created several of the illustrations in this book and combined his efforts with the expertise and talents of Valentart for the remainder.

Valentina is a freelance illustrator and can be found on instagram (valentart_) and fiverr.com

www.ingramcontent.com/pod-product-compliance
Lightning Source LLC
Chambersburg PA
CBHW040516080726
47818CB00016B/282